AF480109

DIVINE PRESCRIPTIONS

Exploring the Spiritual and Medical Benefits

of

WORSHIP

Dr. Paul Atem

Copy-right © 2024 by Dr. Paul Atem

Divine Prescriptions: Exploring the Spiritual and Medical Benefits of Worship

TABLE OF CONTENTS

DEDICATION

This book is dedicated to everyone who cherishes the profound teachings of the word of God. I extend my deepest gratitude to my loving wife, Comfort, whose unwavering support has been my pillar throughout our thirty-three years of marriage. Our daily exploration of the scriptures and shared prayers served as a tremendous source of inspiration to me during the creation of this book.

I am also indebted to our four precious children, Emmanuel, Peace, Favour, and Joshua, for their constant presence and support. Special appreciation goes to Pascaline, our first daughter-in-law, and our cherished grandson, Nathan. Together, we are truly blessed and loving family in Christ.

A sincere appreciation also goes to Dr. Peace Atem in Germany, whose meticulous proofreading enhanced the quality of this book and contributed to its global promotion.

I am grateful to the Rehoboth Centre of Excellence, my church in Nkwen, Bamenda, Cameroon, for providing me with the opportunity to minister occasionally. This platform has played an important role in helping me fulfil God's mandate for my life.

May this book resonate with your spirit and inspire you on your spiritual journey.

INTRODUCTION

This ground-breaking book, examines the spiritual and medical benefits of true worship in straightforward language. All references from the Bible are sourced from the New King James Version (NKJV), and words from Hebrew and Greek are clearly elucidated. The interpretation is rooted in two fundamental principles of the Bible:

Contextual Understanding:

- That is, before interpreting the text, it is essential to comprehend the events preceding the passage and after the passage. This involves reading the pre-text and post-text to situate the context effectively.

Historical Context Exploration:

- In order to grasp the true meaning of the book, it is crucial to delve into the situation at the time the text was written and understand its significance to the people of that era. As we express it, we endeavour to "sit where they sat and hear what they heard."

For instance, the phrase "it's raining cats and dogs" today signifies heavy rain. However, should this expression fade from use with the evolving English language, a potential misunderstanding in the future might interpret it as cats and dogs falling from the sky during rainfall.

Also, in the final chapter, I endeavour to highlight the health benefits of true worship of God. Note that the spiritual and medical advantages synergize, recognizing the tripartite nature of man – body, soul, and spirit because true worship delineates the holistic essence of humanity: God's prized creation.

CHAPTER 1

JESUS TEACHES THE SAMARITAN WOMAN ON TRUE WORSHIP

John 4:1-14, "Therefore, when the Lord knew that the Pharisees had heard that Jesus made and baptized more disciples than John. Vs. 2 – (though Jesus Himself did not baptize, but His disciples), vs. 3- He left Judea and departed again to Galilee.

Vs. 4- But He needed to go through Samaria. Vs. 5- So He came to a city of Samaria which is called Sychar, near the plot of ground that Jacob gave to his son Joseph. Vs. 6 – Now Jacob's well was there. Jesus therefore, being wearied from His journey, sat thus by the well. It was about the sixth hour.

Vs. 7- A woman of Samaria came to draw water. Jesus said to her, "Give Me a drink". Vs. 8- For the disciple had gone away into the city to buy food. Vs. 9- Then the woman of Samaria said to Him, "How is it that you, being a Jew, ask a drink from me, a Samaritan woman?" For the Jews have no dealings with Samaritans.

Vs. 10- Jesus answered and said to her, "if you knew the gift of God, and who it is who says to you, 'Give Me a drink, you would have asked Him, and He would have given you living water". Vs. 11- The woman said to Him, "Sir, you have nothing to draw with, and the well is deep. Where then do you get that living water?

Vs. 12- Are you greater than our father Jacob, who gave us the well, and drank from it himself, as well as his sons and his livestock? Vs. 13- Jesus answered and said to her, "Whoever drinks of this water will thirst again, Vs. 14- but whoever drinks of the water that I shall give him will never thirst. But the water that I shall give him will become in him a fountain of water springing up into everlasting life.

So Jesus changes the narrative from water to living water. From water that never lasts, to water that never runs out. Now let's move down the same chapter as the discourse continues.

John 4:22-23, "You worship what you do not know; we know what we worship, for salvation is of the Jews. Vs. 23- But the hour is coming, and now is, when the true worshippers will worship the Father in spirit and truth; for the Father is seeking *such* to worship Him."

The text says that the Father is seeking "such" or the *"proskynites"* in Greek. This refers to the true worshippers.

John 3:3-8 Jesus answered and said to him, "Most assuredly, I say to you, unless one is born again, he cannot see the kingdom of God." Vs 4 Nicodemus said to Him, "How can a man be born when he is old? Can he enter a second time into his mother's womb and be born?" Vs 5 Jesus answered, "Most assuredly, I say to you, unless one is born of water and the Spirit, he cannot enter the kingdom of God. Vs 6 That which is born of the flesh is flesh, and that which is born of the Spirit is spirit. Vs 7 Do not marvel that I said to you, 'You must be born again.' Vs 8 The wind blows where it wishes, and you hear the sound of it, but cannot tell where it comes from and where it goes. So is everyone who is born of the Spirit."

Jesus speaks in a conceit parable. He uses the wind to talk about the spirit in Chapter 3; then he uses water in Chapter 4 to talk about everlasting life. Jesus keeps changing the narrative from the natural to the spiritual.

Philippians 3:3 NLT *For we who worship by the Spirit of God are the ones who are truly circumcised. We rely on what Christ Jesus has done for us.*

The word of God is truth, and there is reality in it. Also, when you were born again, you were born of the Spirit. Therefore, you must worship God in spirit and reality.

So when it came to worship, He didn't say, go to a particular location or mountain or even to Jerusalem. Instead, he said we should worship in spirit and truth (Reality).

Meaning that worship should go beyond locations and ceremonies i.e. 'kinds and shadows'; rather worship should exist in reality, and the reality of worship is in the spirit.

Worship is also more than just singing a song rather it is simply an opportunity to express worship through singing.

According to the law of first mention, the initial occurrence of the word 'worship' in the Bible is found in Genesis 22. This critical moment transpired when Abraham obeyed God's command by taking Isaac with him to Mount Moriah to present him as an offering on the altar.

In vs. 5; *he said to his servants, "Wait for us here, I and the young lad will go to the mountain to worship and we will come back to you."*

As they embarked on their journey, Abraham and his son were not heading to engage in worship accompanied by a choir, guitars, tambourines, keyboards, or any musical equipment. Yet, this act was called worship, marking the first mention of the word "worship" in the Bible.

According to the law of first mention, when a word makes its first appearance in the Bible, it takes the original essence or meaning of the word.

Another occurrence of the word "worship" is prominently seen in the Gospel of Matthew, chapter 2, where the Bible records the narrative of the wise men who journeyed to pay homage to Jesus.

Remarkably, in their act of worship, the wise men did not arrive adorned with musical instruments; instead, they approached the sacred moment with the most genuine offering of themselves and some sacred items, gold, frankincense, and myrrh. They said, *"We have come from the east to worship"*.

According to the biblical text, when they saw the baby, they walked to where Jesus was in a manger; bowed down and worshipped Him. Although worship is an act from the heart that is expressed in regard, admiration, and devotion, it may also drive you to bow down and kneel; all of these are acts that come from the heart in acknowledgment of all that Christ has done for us.

Our worship of God finds its essence in the revelation of God in a man—Christ. In Christ, we perceive the manifestation of God; shaping the very core of our worship. This process emphasizes the profound connection between the new birth and the transformation of authentic worshippers.

By the transformative experience of the new birth, one naturally becomes a genuine worshipper. Whether or not we choose to vocalize our worship through singing; the act of singing itself does not define worship; rather, it becomes a channel for the expression of the worship that originates from the depth of our renewed being.

In other words, singing becomes a natural outflow of the worship that is already implanted in the material of our reborn existence.

In the temptations of Jesus in Matthew 4. Satan said to Jesus:

Matthew 4:9-10, "And he said to Him, 'All these things I will give You if You will fall down and worship me.' Vs. 10 Then Jesus said to him, 'Away with you, Satan! For it is written, you shall worship the Lord your God, and Him only you shall serve.'"

So Jesus introduces a new reality, and that is the word "**serve.**" You worship the Lord, and only Him shall you serve. In the Greek, the word worship is "*proskyneo*". Then Jesus added the word service – *latreia*.

"You shall worship the Lord your God, and Him only shall you serve". So worship without service is pretence because the worship of God must find expression in the service of God.

As a follower of Christ by nature, you are inherently a true worshipper of God; it is your intrinsic identity. The essence of being born as a worshipper is deeply within you, and it is in the act of worship that we find ourselves serving. Within the realm of worship, we discover the profound dimensions of sacrifice and giving.

Hebrews 13:15-16, "Through him then let us continually offer up a sacrifice of praise to God, that is, the fruit of lips that acknowledge his name. Vs.16 Do not neglect to do good and to share what you have, for such sacrifices are pleasing to God."

However, a question arises: Why do certain individuals exhibit a lack of commitment or consistency in their service to God? This study seeks to unravel the underlying reasons for such inconsistencies.

Romans 12:1-9, "I beseech you therefore, brethren, by the mercies of God, that you present your bodies a living sacrifice, holy, acceptable to God, which is your reasonable service. Vs. 2- And do not be conformed to this world, but be transformed by the renewing of your mind, that you may prove what is that good and acceptable and perfect will of God.

Vs.3 For I say, through the grace given to me, to everyone who is among you, not to think of himself more highly than he ought to think, but to think soberly, as God has dealt to each one a measure of faith.

Vs.4 For as we have many members in one body, but all the members do not have the same function,

Vs.5 So, we, being many, are one body in Christ, and individually members of one another. Vs. 6 Having then gifts differing according to the grace that is given to us, let us use them: if prophecy, let us prophesy in proportion to our faith;

Vs.7 or ministry, let us use it in our ministering; he who teaches, in teaching; Vs.8 he who exhorts, in exhortation; he who gives, with liberality; he who leads, with diligence; he who shows mercy, with cheerfulness. Vs.9 Let love be without hypocrisy. Abhor what is evil. Cling to what is good."

In verses 2 and 3, Paul urges believers to offer their bodies as a living sacrifice, holy and acceptable to God, as part of their legitimate service. He discusses our union and how we are related to one another.

In verses 6-9, we see the expression of our 'body' that has been devoted to God by helping one another. The essence of what Christ does in the life of a believer involves serving God's purpose and serving the body of Christ i.e. serving one another with the gifts that have been bestowed upon us.

So we ought to serve one another and the body of Christ with prophecy, teaching, giving and so on via the anointing (presence and power) of the Spirit. He outlines all of the instruments we use to serve one another since God's objective in giving us His Spirit, is for us to serve His purpose.

You did not receive the Holy Spirit to have a good time; you received it primarily to serve God's purpose in ministry, giving, prophecy etc. That is, service is the highest expression of the Spirit in the believer.

He also says in Vs 9; **let love be without hypocrisy** i.e. let love be genuine.

Now the Bible recorded in Romans 12:10-11, **"Be kindly affectionate to another with brotherly love, in honour giving preference to one another; Vs. 11 not lagging in diligence, fervent in spirit, serving the Lord;"**

So we must have fervency for service. Let's look at other bible translations of Romans 12:11.

Amplified Bible (AMPC): *Never lagging in behind in diligence; aglow in the spirit, enthusiastically serving the Lord.*

The Passion Translation (TPT): *Be enthusiastic to serve the Lord, keeping your passion towards him at boiling hot! Radiate with the glow of the Holy Spirit and let him fill you with excitement as you serve him.*

In other words, we can't be apathetic or lethargic in our service rather we should be excited about serving. There should be a passion or zeal for our service.

A man's zeal for the Lord is impossible to conceal; it radiates through his enthusiastic commitment to the things of God.

So say with me: *"I am aglow for my God and I will serve him with passion!"*

John 14:16-17 AMPC, "And I will ask the Father, and He will give you another Comforter, (Helper, Advocate, Counsellor, Strengthener, and Standby), that He may remain with you forever. Vs. 17 The Spirit of Truth, Whom the world cannot receive (welcome, take to its heart), because it does not see Him nor know and recognise Him. But you know and recognise Him, for He lives with you [constantly] and will be in you."

John had a consistent emphasis on the spirit. It is crucial to recognize that the Spirit of God plays a pivotal role in fostering steadfastness and commitment to service.

The workings of the Spirit, which is directed to your spiritual birth, continue to resonate within your heart, empowering your generation to align with the divine purpose intended for your generation consistently.

In essence, it is the dynamic influence of the Spirit that drives and sustains our relentless dedication to the service of God.

God is actively seeking genuine worshippers who will worship Him in both Spirit and reality. Authentic worship finds its expression in dedicated service to God. A true worshipper radiates with a glowing passion and is fervently devoted to the things of God.

The element of enthusiasm for God's works is unmistakably present in the worshipper's behaviour. This behaviour is the very attitude that the Spirit of God instils in us so that we can wholeheartedly engage in serving Him.

CHAPTER 2

THE TRUE WORSHIP OF GOD IN
THE SYNOPTIC GOSPELS

Let us look closely at the four gospels: Matthew, Mark, Luke, and John, which provide a historical framework for Jesus' life.

Matthew 1:1 The book of the genealogy of Jesus Christ, the son of David, the Son of Abraham

Mark 1:1 The beginning of the gospel of Jesus Christ, the son of God.

Matthew claims that this is the genealogy or genesis of Jesus Christ, which means he is speaking of the 'beginning'. Similarity Mark explores the 'beginning' or origins of the gospel of Christ.

Luke on the other hand, does not start with in the 'beginning' in **Luke 1:1**. But he writes in **Luke 24:27 And beginning at Moses and all the Prophets, He**

expounded to them in all the Scriptures the things concerning Himself. In the text, Jesus is speaking to two disciples on the road to Emmaus after his resurrection. **'All scriptures'** in the text here, refers to the books of Genesis to Malachi of the Old Testament.

However, John started with history. He went straight into the revelation. **John 1:1 In the beginning was the Word, and the Word was with God, and the Word was God.** That is how John commenced his synopsis: In the beginning was the **'logos'**. The word **'logos'** translated from Greek to English means the 'Word'. Although all four gospels touch upon the concept of the beginning but the emphasis in each is slightly different.

John writes a synoptic of the gospel in an epistemological manner just like the others, but his focus, as you will see, was on the after-resurrection effect or the post-resurrection events of Jesus Christ. So, John will speak on the events shortly before Jesus went to the cross and died; as well as the events after his resurrection. And this is why you will see John dedicate John 14 and John 15 to dealing with the post resurrection events.

John 14:2-3 In my father's house are many mansions; if it were not so, I would have told you. I go to prepare a place for you. Vs. 3- And if I go and prepare a place for you, I will come again and receive you to Myself; that where I am, there you may be also.

John also writes in **John 2: 3-4 Now both Jesus and His disciples were invited to the wedding. Vs.3 And when they ran out of wine, the mother of Jesus said to Him, "They have no wine."** This incident marked a pivotal point in John's consistent narrative of the hour, emphasizing the significance of this particular time and the events surrounding it.

John 5:25, Most assuredly, I say to you, the hour is coming, and now is, when the dead will hear the voice of the Son of God; and those who hear will live.

John 7:6 Then Jesus said to them, my time has not yet come, but your time is always ready

John 13:31 So, when he had gone out, Jesus said, "Now the Son of Man is glorified, and God is glorified in Him.

So when Jesus mentioned the hour, it had to do with his death, burial and resurrection, that is when he will be glorified.

John 17:1 Jesus spoke these words, lifted up His eyes to heaven, and said: "Father, the hour has come. Glorify Your Son, that Your Son also may glorify You,

The hour, therefore, refers to his resurrection, it refers to When Jesus rises from the dead. Let us look at what comes with the hour: the gift of the spirit. The giving of the spirit corresponds with his resurrection from the dead.

John 7:37-39 On the last day, that great day of the feast, Jesus stood and cried out, saying, "If anyone thirsts, let him come to Me and drink. Vs.38- He who believes in Me, as the Scripture has said, out of his heart will flow rivers of living water." Vs. 39- But This He spoke concerning the Spirit, whom those believing in Him would receive; for the Holy Spirit was not yet given, because Jesus was not yet glorified.

Furthermore, we may assert that the hour is the moment at which the spirit is bestowed upon us, or it is the moment we receive the gift of eternal life. For instance, we see that the hour is when Jesus is glorified, i.e. raised to honour, when he rose from the dead. So because Jesus was hung on the cross, was buried, and rose triumphantly on the third day, we can say that the hour came and this marks the point at which we attained the position of "sons" of God. In essence, the hour shows the transformative moment in our spiritual journey. Everything will be meaningful when Jesus takes up residence within us, that is when we let him into our lives. So, what precisely will we witness throughout this hour?

Let's see **John 1:12 But as many as received Him, to them He gave the right to become children of God, to those who believe in His name**

Therefore, when Jesus resurrected from the dead, we immediately became the sons and daughters of God. When Jesus came, He was the only begotten son of God but when he died and rose, he became the First begotten from the dead: the prototype of what we become after salvation. *So* we are God's sons and were born of God as a result of his resurrection. The resurrection also occurs when we are baptized in the Spirit. With the resurrection, spiritual baptism became a reality.

John 1:32-33 **And John bore witness, saying, "I saw the Spirit descending from heaven like a dove, and He remained upon Him. Vs. 33- I did not know Him, but He who sent me to baptize with water said to me, 'Upon whom you see the Spirit descending and remaining on Him, this is He who baptizes with the Holy Spirit.'** Jesus does not baptize with water. He baptizes today with the Holy Ghost. But observe that in the conversation he had in chapter 4 of John with the Samaritan woman at the well.

John 4:19-22 The woman said to Him, "Sir, I perceive that You are a prophet. Vs.20- Our fathers worshiped on this mountain and you Jews say in Jerusalem is the place where one ought to worship." Vs.21- Jesus said to her, "woman, believe Me, the hour is coming when you will neither on this mountain, nor in Jerusalem, worship the Father. Vs. 22- You worship what you do not know; we know what we worship, for Salvation is of the Jews. Salvation is of the Jews, or the saviour is a Jew, signifying that the chosen redeemer belongs to the

Jewish lineage. It conveys the idea that the saviour is inherently a Jew. However, it is essential to emphasize that this concept does not imply an imperative for individuals to physically journey to Israel and acquire the title of Rabbi, nor does it suggest a mandate to adopt or strictly adhere to Jewish ordinances and practices. The essence lies in recognizing the historical and cultural context without necessitating a wholesale adoption of outward aspects.

Now let's look at vs. 23 again. **John 4:23-24 But the hour is coming and now is, when the true worshipers will worship the Father in Spirit and truth; for the Father is seeking such to worship Him. Vs.24- God is Spirit, and those who worship Him must worship in Spirit and truth.** We should take note of authentic worshippers who will worship the Father in spirit and truth (reality).

God is Spirit, and those who worship Him must do so in spirit and truth. God is Spirit not a spirit. **'A Spirit'** does not appear in the original text. Rather it says **God is Spirit**, and those who worship Him must do so both in spirit and truth.

It is obvious when Paul went into Athens, there were several shrines all over the city and different churches, with the inscription on the building *'To the unknown God'*. Paul told the Athenians **'you worship; you know not what'.** But if you are going to worship God, you must worship in spirit and truth. The hour cometh, when the "true worshipers", not just worshipers; but the "true worshippers" (John 4:24) must worship him in spirit and truth. Therefore, worshippers cannot determine how to worship, and worshippers cannot dictate the manner in which they desire to worship. Worship is not subject to the discretion of the worshiper; instead, the worshipped (God) has established the parameters for authentic worship that leads to Him. It is critical that, in the worship of God, individuals must adhere to the requirement of worshipping Him in spirit and truth or in spirit and in reality. This truth stands in contrast to ceremonial practices, such as worship on specific mountains or temple worship, with its types and shadows. None of these ceremonial forms constitutes genuine worship.

True worship, in spirit and truth, surpasses shadows and ceremonies, rather it's about finding reality in the authentic experience of the Spirit.

In **John 4:16-24. Jesus said to her, "Go, call your husband, and come here." Vs. 17- The woman answered and said, "I have no husband." Jesus said to her, "You have well said, 'I have no husband,' vs. 18-for you have had five husbands, and the one whom you now have is not your husband; in that you spoke truly." Vs.19- The woman said to Him ,"Sir, I perceive that You are a prophet.Vs.20- Our fathers worshiped on this mountain and you Jews say that in Jerusalem is the place where one ought to worship." Vs.21- Jesus said to her, "Woman, believe Me , the hour is coming when you will neither on this mountain, nor in Jerusalem, worship the Father.**

Vs. 22- You worship what you do not know; we know what we worship, for Salvation is of the Jews.Vs.23- But the hour is coming and now is, when the true worshipers will worship the Father in Spirit and truth; for the Father is seeking such to worship Him. Vs.24- God is Spirit, and those who worship Him must worship in spirit and truth.

In Vs. 22 we see that salvation is of the Jews or the Saviour is a Jew. While in Vs.24, it says, "God is spirit", meaning He is the source of life, yet invisible to mankind, and those who worship him must worship him in Spirit and in truth. In "truth" means in "reality."

John 14:16-17 AMPC And I will ask the Father, and He will give you another Comforter, (Helper, Advocate, Counsellor, Strengthener, and Standby), that He may remain with you forever. Vs. 17 The Spirit of Truth, Whom the world cannot receive (welcome, take to its heart), because it does not see Him nor know and recognise Him. But you know and recognise Him, for He lives with you [constantly] and will be in you.

In fact, one of the designations of the Holy Ghost (*Pneuma to Hagion*) is that He the revealer of the truth cos He is the spirit of truth.

John 16:12-13; I still have many things to say to you, but you cannot bear them now. Vs.13 However, when He, the Spirit of truth, has come, He will guide you into all truth; for He will not speak on His own authority, but whatever He hears He will speak; and He will tell you things to come

So when Christ says we worship in the spirit and in truth; the truth is found in the spirit, the reality of the spirit of truth is in Christ.

It is said of Jesus in **John 1:9 That was the true Light which gives light to every man coming into the world.** So Christ is the true light that lights every man that cometh into the world. In **John 5:35 And Jesus said to them, I am the bread of life. He who comes to Me shall never hunger, and he who believes in Me shall never thirst.** John spoke of Jesus, affirming that Jeus was the true light, who embodies the ultimate truth. The true reality is exclusively found in Christ, as he declared, "**I am the way, the truth, and the light**," indicating that he is the embodiment of reality itself. The truth is another of Christ, and which is synonymous with the word Amen, signifying faithfulness and truth.

So when Christ says, "the hour cometh," He is implying His forthcoming death, burial, and resurrection, which serve as the means of our redemption. His resurrection is undertaken on our behalf, and His ascension is not a physical ascent into space but a spiritual entrance into our hearts. His purpose was to establish a dwelling place within the hearts of humanity and to facilitate a union between man and God. When Christ died, was buried, rose and ascended, the ascension was a spiritual journey into our hearts. "The hour cometh, and now is," He conveyed to the woman, indicating the immediacy and relevance of the transformative process.

John 4:21 *Jesus said to her, Woman, believe Me, the hour is coming when you will neither on this mountain, nor in Jerusalem, worship the Father*

"Not in Jerusalem nor on this mountain," is the background of the narrative. The Samaritans resided and worshipped God on their mountain, whereas the Jews insisted that Jerusalem was the designated place for worship. However, Jesus went beyond both perspectives, declaring that worship is not limited to either mountain or city – "Neither on this mountain nor in Jerusalem" – signifying equality, denying any advantage to one group over the other.

Jesus emerges as the great balance, dismantling ideas of superiority or inferiority. The bone of contention was temple worship; Moses, on the other hand, conveyed a New Testament truth through types and shadows and presented the Jews with temple worship. They embraced it based on their understanding of the Torah.

Jesus now proclaimed that there would be no necessity to go to the temple for worship. The hour cometh expresses that the time is approaching when authentic worshippers will engage in worship in spirit and reality, transcending the symbols of adoration associated with temple worship. In their cultural context, temple worship involved various acts of obeisance – kissing, kneeling, bowing down, falling, and paying homage. But worship encompasses more than these acts.

Because worship involves rendering service and showing obeisance before a higher authority, a practice reserved for God alone. Jesus exemplified this in the garden of Gethsemane when he knelt, turning an act from the heart into a lifestyle—a continual expression of worship.

"Worship", as demonstrated by Jesus, emanates from the heart. A genuine worshipper pays homage, shows respect, and honours God sincerely. True worship is not a mere ritual but a way of life—a dedicated and respectful lifestyle emanating from a heart wholly devoted to God.

Matthew 15:8-9 These people draw near to Me with their mouth and honour Me with their lips but their heart is far from Me. Vs. 9- And in vain they worship Me, Teaching as doctrines the commandments of men."

True worship is the sincere act of reverencing God with a heart wholly devoted to Him. It goes beyond mere rituals; it is a service emanating from a heart that belongs entirely to God. True worship is the profound reverence of God, fuelled by the spirit of God dwelling within a person.

CHAPTER 3

TRUE WORSHIP

(*As Illustrated By The Wise Men*)

Matthew 2:1-12 Now after Jesus was born in Bethlehem of Judea in the days of Herod the king, behold, wise men from the East came to Jerusalem, saying, "Where is He who has been born King of the Jews? For we have seen His star in the East and have come to worship Him. Vs.3 When Herod the king heard this, he was troubled, and all Jerusalem with him. Vs. 4 And when he had gathered all the chief priests and scribes of the people together, he inquired of them where the Christ was to be born. Vs.5 So they said to him, "In Bethlehem of Judea, for thus it is written by the prophet: Vs.6 'But you, Bethlehem, in the land of Judah, Are not the least among the rulers of Judah; For out of you shall come a Ruler Who will shepherd My people Israel'." Vs. 7 Then Herod, when he had secretly called the wise men, determined from them what time the star appeared. Vs.8 And he sent them to Bethlehem and said, "Go and search carefully for the young Child, and when you have found Him, bring back word to me, that I may come and worship Him also." Vs.9 When they heard the King, they departed; and behold, the star which they had seen in the East went before them, till it came and stood over where the young Child was. Vs. 10 When they saw the star, they rejoiced with exceedingly great joy. Vs.11 And when they had come into the house, they saw the young Child with Mary His mother, and fell down and worshiped Him. And when they had opened their treasures, they presented gifts to Him: gold, frankincense, and myrrh. Vs. 12 Then, being divinely warned in a dream that they should not return to Herod, they departed for their own country another way.

When Jesus was born, a group of wise men travelled from the East to Bethlehem to honour him. These wise men were knowledgeable scientists; they were astronomers who had studied the stars, and they understood events from studying the stars. They were called the magic–wise men. They were not magicians; they were truly people who could use their scientific knowledge to predict what had happened or what could happen. Today, meteorologists, study clouds and temperatures in order to predict the weather.

If you were in the USA or Europe now, suppose you have an event, let's say a wedding in March. The selection of the date would be contingent on the weather forecast for that day as part of your wedding planning. For instance, if you initially considered the 15th of March and the weather forecast predicts rain in the morning, you might opt for the 25th of March, where the forecast promises sunshine throughout the day.

This insight is derived not from revelation but from scientific knowledge. So the weather forecasts, provides precise information about the weather conditions for a given day. Also, for example; if the forecast indicates rain at 2 p.m., it will commence raining precisely at that time, regardless of the bright sunlight earlier in the day.

In the story of the wise men, they engaged in the scientific study of stars and planets, enabling them to ascertain with precision that the birth of Jesus had occurred due to the presence of an unusual star. Through their careful observations and research, they could tell with scientific precision that a king has been born. Subsequently, they embarked on a journey, following the star and moving westward to worship the new born king.

Upon reaching Jerusalem, instead of continuing to follow the star, they proceeded directly to the palace of King Herod. Their reasoning led them to believe that a baby king would be born in the palace of the reigning king, King Herod the Great. They informed King Herod: "We know a baby king has been born; we have seen his star in the East, and we have come to worship him."

In verse 3, it is noted that when Herod heard this, he was greatly disturbed, and the entire city of Jerusalem was worried as well. When individuals hold political power, they are often reluctant to entertain the prospect of someone else assuming their position. Kings typically retain their power until they pass it on to their sons or daughters, only after their death. Herod's disturbance is emphasized in verse 4 and verse 5. He called all the priests and scribes, and anxiously asked them where the Christ (The **Messiah**; the anointed one) was to be born.

They replied that he was to be born in Bethlehem of Judea for this is what is written by the prophet Micah and they quoted from **Micah 5:2 "But you, Bethlehem Ephrathah, though you are little among the thousands of Judah, yet out of you shall come forth to Me The One to be Ruler in Israel, whose goings forth are from of old, From everlasting."** Same as in verse 6 of **Matthew 2.**

The story continues in **Matthew 2:7-8 AMP** *Then Herod secretly sent for the magi and learned from them the [exact] time that the star [had first] appeared. Vs. 8 Then he sent them to Bethlehem, saying, "Go and search carefully for the Child; when you have found Him, report to me, so that I too may come and worship Him."*

Some people may speak about following Jesus, but their actions don't match their words, and their hearts are far from Him. We see later in **Matthew 2:16-18**, that Herod eventually tried to harm Jesus. He went to extreme lengths, even killing many babies aged two years and below.

Vs 16 Then Herod, when he saw that he was deceived by the wise men, was exceedingly angry; and he sent forth and put to death all the male children who were in Bethlehem and in all its districts, from two years old

and under, according to the time which he had determined from the wise men. Vs 17 Then was fulfilled what was spoken by Jeremiah the prophet, saying:

Vs 18 "A voice was heard in Ramah,

Lamentation, weeping, and great mourning,

Rachel weeping for her children,

Refusing to be comforted,

Because they are no more."

Despite his efforts, he couldn't find Jesus because Jesus was hidden in Africa, specifically in Egypt.

Matthew 2:13 NLT After the wise men were gone, an angel of the Lord appeared to Joseph in a dream. "Get up! Flee to Egypt with the child and his mother," the angel said. "Stay there until I tell you to return, because Herod is going to search for the child to kill him."

I believe that this story highlights something profound about God's plan for Africa – it's a place of protection and preservation. Jesus, the Son of God, found safety in Africa, emphasizing the importance of the continent in preserving life.

Another lesson from the story is to withhold your vision until it matures before sharing it. Whether it's a business idea or any concept, develop it thoroughly before revealing it. Premature exposure of your plans may invite interference or sabotage from jealous individuals who might try to undermine or destroy them. The wise men, in sharing their vision and the purpose of their visit—to worship a new born baby king—faced the determined opposition of Herod, who sought to eliminate the threat to his reign by plotting the child's death. Herod's jealousy of an infant reflected his desire to maintain sole power for many more years. So exercise caution and refrain from disclosing your God given plans until they are fully developed or with the right individuals. Consider how many people today engage in pretense, worshipping God with their lips or singing for God while harbouring evil in their hearts.

After leaving King Herod palace, the wise men continued to follow the star until it led them to Bethlehem where Jesus was born.

Question: Why did they not continue to follow the star or why did they think that a king must be born in a king's palace? Let's find out why

The answer lies in the inherent limitation of human knowledge when it is detached from God. No matter how highly learned you are, without Christ, your understanding is restrained. Your choices can easily be misguided. While you may possess knowledge, the absence of Christ in your life can lead to erroneous decisions. It's a reminder that, without Christ, even the most educated minds may deviate off course. Thankfully, the wise men eventually came to realize the need to continue following the star.

In **Matthew 2:11**; the wise men got to Bethlehem, they entered the house and saw the baby Jesus with Mary his mother and they bowed down and worshipped him. Then opening their gifts; they presented to Him gifts of **Gold, Frankincense** and **Myrrh**, 3 gifts. Now I want you to know that the bible never said three wise men: we do not know the number of wise men. The bible just said wise men from the east in plural; so they could have been three or more. But why do we usually say three wise men? It's because of the 3 gifts; **Gold, Frankincense** and **Myrrh**.

1. **Gold:** Is it not a precious metal befitting for kings? Gold is one of the rarest naturally –occurring elements in the Earth's crust. Hence throughout history, we often see kings or rulers being associated with or presented with gold or golden objects because of their revered status in their kingdoms. Even bourgeois individuals i.e. very wealthy persons, prefer to store their wealth in the form of gold rather than banknotes. In some cases, a country's currency may be backed by the amount of gold it possesses. Gold does not depreciate in value whereas bank notes do depreciate in value and true wealth lies in preserving assets through tangible investments. Those who understand the enduring value of wealth often choose gold reserves. In a symbolic gesture, the wise men presented gold to Jesus, signifying his royal status as the King of kings and the Lord of lords. This act serves as a timeless reminder that true riches transcend the ephemeral nature of currency.

2. **Frankincense:** Frankincense held a significant role in the temple, serving as a fragrant and precious perfume during prayers. The act of presenting Frankincense to Jesus symbolized the idea that, through Jesus, our prayers ascend to God like a delightful fragrance. This

signifies that when we pray in Jesus' name, our petitions find favour with God, resulting in answered prayers.

3. **Myrrh:** Myrrh was used for the embalming of the dead, similar to formalin. By presenting myrrh, the wise men conveyed the message that Jesus was destined to die and serve as the sacrificial offering for our sins. He was not merely going to pay the price; he was going to be the price, the ultimate sacrifice for our sins. Jesus' death was to usher us into eternal union with God, leading us into genuine worship. This worship transcended the symbolic and shadowy practices of the Old Testament, as his death and resurrection brought us into true worship in spirit and truth (reality).

The reality of Jesus' sacrifice is evident in his death and subsequent resurrection, symbolizing an ascent into our hearts. This transformative process allows us to become the righteousness of God in Christ and transforms us into the living temple of God, as God now resides within us.

So, worship involves sacrificial giving. The wise men exemplified this in their act of worship, giving not just gifts but offering what truly cost them. It is a lesson for us to embrace sacrificial giving as a genuine act of worship.

Contrary to the notion of giving in church for the expectation of God's blessings, our giving should be an expression of gratitude for the blessings already bestowed upon us through Christ's sacrifice. Christ sacrificially gave his life for us, and our giving should be a response to that selfless act.

Some prosperity preachers claim that giving a specific amount, such as a particular amount of dollars, in the church will result in God multiplying it and blessing the giver with a significant return. However, these assertions often misquote scripture and promote an uneven understanding of the true essence of giving.

The typically quote: ***"Give, and it shall be given unto you: good measure, press down, shaken together, and running over, shall men give into your bosom..."*** from **Luke 6:38 KJV**. The mentioned scripture doesn't revolve around offerings or giving within the church; rather, it emphasizes giving and receiving among people in a social context.

So when you contribute in a church setting, it is an act of worship devoid of expectations. If financial gain is what you seek, the avenue is through employment or engaging in a business venture. God can utilize your work or business as a conduit for blessings. Uphold diligence, and prosperity will follow. Sow seeds in your personal pursuits — like farming — and watch your efforts yield crops that can be sold for profit. We should feel free to invest or create revenue streams and if you're uncertain about what type of business to pursue, seek advice from seasoned entrepreneurs or attend a reputable business school for guidance. Armed with knowledge, embark on the right business venture, and success will likely follow. We should give generously to God as an expression of worship, anticipating nothing in return. And later, when you prosper, return to God with gratitude, still expecting nothing in return. After all, the essence of true worship lies in giving, mirroring God's nature as a generous provider, now ingrained in you as a believer in Christ. Remember, **John 3:16 "For God so loved the world that he gave..."**

In **Matthew 2:12 Then, being divinely warned in a dream that they should not return to Herod, they departed for their own country another way.** We see that the wise men obeyed the spirit of God. Worship is connected to obedience, specifically obedience to the prompting of the Holy Spirit. It is crucial to cultivate the ability to sense the direction of the Spirit of God in you. Take the time to adjust your ears to His modest whispers and prompts.

Additionally, mastering the art of communication with God through prayer is fundamental to deepening your connection with the divine spirit of God. By actively engaging in a two-way conversation with God, you not only express your reverence but also open yourself to profound insights and divine wisdom. Therefore, make it a priority to not only offer your worship through obedience but also to enable a dynamic and meaningful relationship with the Creator through prayerful communication.

In conclusion when the wise men came to adore Jesus as an infant, they brought presents, making worship concrete. Worship is not just simply what you say; it is also about what you do. So, worship is an act. The wise men from the East brought presents to worship and then bowed down to worship; they recognized who Jesus was while worshipping. They worshipped Jesus as a king. It goes beyond that; as they were about to return to Herod, the angel of the Lord advised them not to do so, and they obeyed, demonstrating that adoration is backed up by obedience because obedience is the substance of true worship. That is why worship is not just a song; because worship is in our nature, our DNA; we are born again as true worshippers, so we live in obedience to the word of God.

CHAPTER 4

SPIRITUAL APATHY IS INCOMPATIBLE WITH TRUE WORSHIP

Colossians 1:9-10: For this reason, we also, since the day we heard it, do not cease to pray for you, and to ask that you may be filled with the knowledge of His will in all wisdom and spiritual understanding; Vs.10 that you may walk worthy of the Lord, fully pleasing Him, being fruitful in every good work and increasing in the knowledge of God.

Paul the Apostle writing to the Colossians says his prayer is that we be fruitful in every good work. We ought to be fruitful in our Christian walk. The question you want to ask yourself is: 'am I really producing fruits or am I really a fruitful believer?'

Ephesians 2:8-9 For by grace you have been saved through faith, and that not of yourselves; it is the gift of God, Vs.9 not of works, lest anyone should boast.

Jesus saved me; He paid the price for my sins, granted me eternal life, and I am secured in Christ. However, the critical question remains: am I fruitful? And does the quality of the fruit I bear align with the quality of the seed sown in my life? These are deeply personal inquiries — questions that each follower of Christ should be earnestly contemplating by now.

The purpose of the Gospel is to bring people to a saving knowledge of Jesus Christ, and the purpose of the local church is to establish them in Christ by teaching them God's word so that they can grow in Christ.

Ephesians 2:10 For we are His workmanship, created in Christ Jesus for good works, which God prepared beforehand that we should walk in them.

So, there are good works we are supposed to walk in; we are redeemed and saved by Jesus unto good works and this implies that there are specific works or actions we ought to engage in actively.

In this context, "**WALK**" indicates that God expects us to be proactive. James reinforces this idea by stating that '**faith without works is dead' (James 2:17)**, emphasizing the importance of our actions in service to others after experiencing salvation.

In Colossians, Paul fervently prayed that believers should be fruitful, producing fruits worthy of the divine call upon their lives. In biblical terms, fruitlessness is equated with spiritual apathy. Therefore, striving to bear fruits aligned with God's purpose is not merely an option but a vital aspect of our spiritual journey.

Romans 12:11 NLT Never be lazy, but work hard and serve the Lord enthusiastically.

There is a phenomenon known as spiritual apathy, and the phenomenon is precisely what Paul addressed in Romans 12:11. This implies that, as a Christian with the Holy Spirit within you, it is possible to be sluggish or indifferent. What does it mean to lack enthusiasm in your endeavours? It denotes a sense of indifference and unconcern, where there is no genuine excitement about your actions. You may find yourself singing, preaching, or dancing without a heartfelt connection to the purpose behind these activities. Whether people come to Christ or not, the state of empty seats at churches or the status of bills involved in the spreading of the gospel being paid becomes inconsequential to you. Apathy leads to mere motions without genuine emotions, indicative of a lack of concern, commitment, and passion.

Interestingly, even in this state of apathy, one may still attend church and engage in activities such as preaching, singing or protocol duties. Titles might be adopted not for the sake of fulfilling responsibilities but rather for the respect associated with them. They may crave accolades but shy away from the responsibilities inherent in carrying those titles because they seek only the glory tied to titles without being invested in the stories that lead to such glory.

In the book of Revelation, John records Jesus speaking to the seven churches in Asia. The important thing about the letters to the seven churches is that he addressed the seven churches differently. Each church received a unique message from Jesus, tailored to its specific context. The instructions from God varied according to the needs and circumstances of each congregation. The angel of the church, serving as the messenger of the local church, was entrusted with giving these instructions to the congregation.

The concept of the local church is not a human invention; rather, it is God's plan for the nourishment and preservation of His people. God intentionally places believers within a local church family to facilitate their learning of the sound teachings of His Word within a supportive environment enabling you to fulfil the purpose God has for your life. The local church stands as one of the greatest gifts from God for our lives. It serves as a place where you receive essential instructions upon which to build your life as a follower of Christ.

So Jesus spoke specifically to the seven churches where he ended all the letters with, **'He who has an ear, let him hear what the Spirit is saying to the seven churches'.** There are messages in those letters that we need to pay attention to but let's look at a particular church among the seven: the church in Laodicea.

Revelation 3:14-16 And to the angel of the church of the Laodiceans write, 'These things says the Amen, the Faithful and True Witness, the Beginning of the creation God: Vs.15 "I know your works, that you are neither cold nor hot. I could wish you were cold or hot.

Vs.16 So then, because you are lukewarm, and neither cold nor hot, I will vomit you out of My mouth.

I know your works; you are neither cold nor hot; you have entered a state of apathy, and I will spit you out of my mouth. You better be cold or hot. In this context, the speaker is not addressing matters of salvation but rather engaging with believers. The focus is on the works of the believer. "I know your works, I know your ministry, I know you; your service to me is to make yourself known, not for God to be seen in you. I know you are born again; I know you are serving me, but you are neither hot nor cold. You preach but yet, you not truly passionate about the salvation of souls; you're lukewarm."

So, I will spew you out of my mouth. I would even prefer that you are cold. Guess what, God even prefers cold to lukewarm! You might think lukewarm is better than being cold, but God says it is even better for you to be cold than to be neither cold nor hot.

In **Rev.3:15** was implying that the Laodicean church is lukewarm, and the Laodiceans completely understood the message.

To understand what the Laodiceans understood, let's picture sitting where they sat and listening to what they heard.

Laodicea was situated between two large cities. One city was named Heropolis, while the other was named Colossae. So Laodicea was located midway between Heropolis and Colossae.

Colossae was a city with a very tall mountain named Catmos. There was usually snow on the pinnacle of Catmos Mountain. Springs flowed from the high mountain into Colossae, bringing extremely cold water. So the water that poured down from the mountain into Colossae was ice cold, wonderfully refreshing.

Herapolis was in striking antithesis to Colossae. Herapolis was a low-lying location that was quite hot. Because the city had earthquakes formed springs known as hot springs which are springs produced by the emergence of geothermally heated groundwater onto the surface of the Earth. In other words, the water from the springs were heated. So, during the frigid winter months, people came to Herapolis to enjoy the hot springs. And in hot weather, they went to Colossae to drink cold, refreshing water.

At the time, some people believed that hot spring water had medicinal properties. So, individuals suffering from chronic ailments such as diabetes or cancer, would go to Herapolis to drink the hot spring water with the hope of getting healed.

But Laodicea was in the middle of these two towns. The Laodiceans were wealthy; they had the money to get cold water from Catmos Mountain in Colossae and transport it to Laodicea. However, due to the distance, by the time the water travelled from Colossae to Laodicea, it had turned lukewarm, neither cold nor hot. Lukewarm water is unpleasant, unfit for drinking, and not refreshing. When the Laodiceans tried to drink the water, they spit it out because the objective of giving it to them had been defeated. That water was unpleasant, undrinkable, and lukewarm; it was neither cold nor hot. So that water was pointless. When Jesus informed the Laodiceans that they were useless and that He would spit them out of His mouth, they understood the communication from the lukewarm water that they had in their country.

To be lukewarm means that your service is ineffective to God, but you can appear to be serving Him. A lukewarm individual can even create a church, but the goal of such a church is not to bring others to salvation and build their lives on solid doctrine. Remember that, the primary purpose of a church should solely be to lead people to a profound understanding of Christ, facilitating salvation, and to nurture them through the solid teachings found in the Word of God—nothing more. Anything beyond the mission of bringing individuals to Christ and grounding them in sound doctrine constitutes a divergence into another gospel, a luke-warmness that manifests as a mere public display of ourselves, devoid of any eternal value.

Engaging in any public display that does not contribute to bringing people to Christ or fostering their growth in sound teaching is not aligned with the essence of Christ; it epitomizes luke-warmness. Luke-warm services rendered to God amount to works that are unrefreshing, tasteless, and essentially worthless. It is imperative to recognize the quality of our service to God; a lukewarm service, lacking fervour and dedication, holds no real value.

Let us be vigilant in ensuring that our actions within the church are purposeful, focusing on the eternal impact of leading others to Christ and nurturing them with the profound teachings of the Word of God. Anything less than this risks diluting the true essence of our service and depriving it of the transformative power it should possess.

So Christ is warning the church in **Rev. 3:19 AMP Those whom I [dearly and tenderly] love, I rebuke and discipline [showing them their faults and instructing them]; so be enthusiastic and repent.**

What is the Spirit of God communicating to us as a church? The message is clear: "Wake up from your *spiritual slumber* and be zealous in His service".

Ephesians 5:14 Therefore He says:

"Awake, you who sleep,

Arise from the dead,

And Christ will give you light."

In this appeal, the call is to rouse any spiritual indifference or complacency that might have sneaked in. The imagery of awakening and arising carries a sense of urgency, emphasizing the need for renewed zeal and vibrancy in our commitment to God's service. By answering this call, believers are invited to embrace spiritual life and the illuminating light that Christ provides when we are fully awakened and engaged in His purpose.

CHAPTER 5

FALSE WORSHIP IN THE TOWER OF BABEL

Gen 11:1-9 Now the whole earth had one language and one speech. Vs.2- And it came to pass, as they journeyed from the east, that they found a plain in the land of Shinar, and they dwelt there. Vs. 3-Then they said to one another, "Come, let us make bricks and bake *them* thoroughly." They had brick for stone, and they had asphalt for mortar. Vs.4- And they said, "Come, let us build ourselves a city, and a tower whose top is in the heavens; let us make a name for ourselves, lest we be scattered abroad over the face of the whole earth." Vs.5- But the Lord came down to see the city and the tower which the sons of men had built. Vs.6- And the Lord said, "Indeed the people are one and they all have one language, and this is what they begin to do; now nothing that they propose to do will be withheld from them. Vs.7- Come, let Us go down and there confuse their language, that they may not understand one another 's speech." Vs.8-So the Lord scattered them

abroad from there over the face of all the earth, and they ceased building the city. Vs.9- Therefore its name is called Babel, because there the Lord confused the language of all the earth; and from there the Lord scattered them abroad over the face of all the earth.

Genesis 11 presents a singular narrative often referred to as the Tower of Babel. Upon studying the book of Genesis, one must recognize the prevalence of counter-narratives or opposites throughout its content. Genesis is rich with such instances, and we can explore a few of these counter-narratives:

1. The earth without form or void – the spirit of God moved on the surface of the earth

2. Darkness – Light

3. Seed of the serpent – Seed of the woman

4. Cain – Abel

Having just examined Genesis 11, if we advance to Genesis 12, focusing on the call of Abraham, a remarkable contrast arises. Genesis 12 stands as the precise opposite of Genesis 11, particularly the Tower of Babel narrative. This counter-narrative or opposition between Genesis 11 and Genesis 12 highlights the intricate pattern of contrasts woven throughout the book of Genesis.

Genesis 11:4 And they said, "come, let us build ourselves a city, and a tower whose top is in the heavens; *let us make a name for ourselves,* **lest we be scattered abroad over the face of the whole earth."** I used to believe that what these people were attempting to do was construct a skyscraper, an exceptionally tall building intended to reach the heavens and challenge God. Consequently, God intervened and brought their efforts to a halt.

Gen 11:5-9 But the Lord came down to see the city and the tower which the sons of men had built. Vs.6- And the Lord said, "In deed the people are one and they all have one language, and this is what they begin to do; now nothing that they propose to do will be withheld from them.

Vs.7- come, let Us go down and there confuse their language, that they may not understand one another speech." Vs.8-So the Lord scattered them abroad from there over the face of all the earth, and they ceased

building the city. Vs.9- Therefore its name is called Babel, because there the Lord confused the language of all the earth; and from there the Lord scattered them abroad over the face of all the earth.

Take note of *"let us make us a name"*. The word 'name', from the Hebrew is the word *'Shem'*. It means, let us make for us what is popular. This expression signifies an intention to establish recognition or it suggests the collective decision to become well-known and acknowledged. In essence, the notion is to create a reputation or identity that aligns with being popular.

Gen 4:17 And Cain knew his wife, and she conceived and bore Enoch. And he built a city, and called the name of the city after the name of his son- Enoch.

In the Old Testament, a name serves as a symbolic representation of a function or an action to be carried out. In the context of Genesis, a name signifies something tangible, something worthy of worship, or a future identity one aspires to attain. This contextual interpretation sheds light on the significance of names within the passage we are examining.

Gen 4:26 And as for Seth, to him also a son was born; and he named him Enosh. Then men began to call on the name of the Lord. Then began men to call upon the name of the Lord. To call upon the name of the Lord, means to worship God.

In **Genesis 11:4 And they said, "come, let us build ourselves a city, and a tower whose top is in the heavens; let us make a name for ourselves, lest we be scattered abroad over the face of the whole earth."**

These people began building a city and a tower. To understand what they were doing, let's return to the basic principles of Bible interpretation:

1. When studying a Bible text or chapter, in order to understand the context of what you're reading, read the text before (the pretext) and then after the text (the post text).

2. Put yourself in their place i.e. sit where they sat and listen to what they heard to locate the context.

When these people heard "tower," they did not envision a high-rise building. The concept of a tower, in their understanding, did not involve a structure reaching the sky like a skyscraper. Instead, a tower represented a designated space for worship, a place for deities, and a setting for the reverence of gods.

Therefore, when they spoke of building a tower unto heaven, the emphasis wasn't solely on its physical height. Rather, it was an endeavour to establish a space for worshipping a deity or a god. In our contemporary understanding, the term "tower" may evoke thoughts of tall buildings. However, in their cultural context, a tower was essentially a place created for religious worship.

This concept bears similarity to but is not identical to, a temple—a place for worshipping deities or gods. So, when they expressed the desire to build a tower unto heaven, the intention went beyond mere elevation; it aimed at creating a place of worship and making a name for themselves or, in other words, establishing a space for worship and achieving renown. Modern rockets and other advanced technologies of mankind cannot physically ascend into heaven. How, then, could one imagine the idea that in the Genesis narrative, people attempted to construct a tower to reach the heavens?

The Tower of Babel, as illustrated in Genesis, symbolizes more than just a futile architectural endeavour, rather it serves as a representation of idol worship.

In **Genesis 4:26** Men began to call upon the name of the Lord, engaging in worship and devotion to God. However, in Genesis 11, a counter-narrative emerged. Men declared their refusal to worship the Lord God any longer. They intended to construct a place of worship, not for God, but for themselves. The objective was clear: to make a name for themselves and to indulge in self-idolization—a form of humanistic worship and self-adulation.

The Tower of Babel, in this context, symbolizes a site of self-worship, deviating from the universal blessings and the exaltation of God's name throughout the earth. The individuals in Genesis 11 rejected the idea of making the name of the Lord great in all the Earth. Instead, they opted to cease making God popular and to, in turn, focus on making themselves renowned. Their decision manifested in the construction of the Tower of Babel—a monument to their self-centred worship.

The shift was from worshipping God to worshipping themselves, as they sought popularity not for God but for their name. In this act, the Tower of Babel becomes a symbol of forsaking the worship of God to indulge in self-worship and self-promotion.

The word Babel comes from the Hebrew word *'Balal'*. It appears 262 times in the Old Testament. It is the origin of the word Babylonia. The term *'Balal'* or **Babylon** refers to a combination. It means to combine worship of God with other activities. So, the people in Genesis 11 knew exactly what they were doing. They weren't ignorant. They said, 'Let's do it for ourselves. We've worshipped God enough in Genesis 4, so let's stop. Enough with the worship of God; let us now do it for ourselves.'

This is idol worship in Genesis 11 which is a counter narrative to the true worship of God in Genesis 4 where human beings commenced calling upon the name of the Lord in worship. However, in Genesis 11, a shift occurred. They proclaimed, "No more; we won't worship God again. Let us worship ourselves."

Now, it's crucial to understand that idol worship takes various forms. When we mention idol worship, one might envision a singular image in a designated space — perhaps a shrine; whether known or hidden, where people kneel and worship. This perception is often associated with some societies or regions in the world. Yet, idol worship, in essence, encompasses anything to which you direct your worship. It goes beyond physical images in a shrine, extending to any object, concept, or even self-worship that becomes the focal point of devotion.

Anything you value more than God's worship or anything you admire and value more than God. And this term *anything* may represent: people, objects, ideas, money, or desires. Some people even adore science. Rather than using science to attain a noble goal, they idolize it. They claim I don't care what God's word says; I care what men discover.

The narrative of Genesis 11 'let us establish a name for ourselves' is the conception or commencement of Babylon; idol worship, where people begin to worship all types of things and multiply servitude to objects.

Multiply service to objects, multiply servitude to people: Babylon, whereas the entire earth should worship a single God. If you read further in Gen 12, it is the exact opposite of Genesis 11. In Gen 12, someone who was an idol worshipper by the name of Abraham was called to a land where he would abandon idol worship and worship the Almighty God.

The unity of Genesis 11 was idol worship. In Genesis 12, there is also another unity: faith in God, the true worship of God. The worship of God in Genesis 12 is the exact opposite of the idol worship in Genesis 11. So as we delve deeper into Genesis 12, a stark contrast emerges when compared to Genesis 11. This contrast underscores the counter-narrative nature of the book of Genesis.

Abraham, initially an idol worshipper, is called to a land where he forsakes idol worship and turns to worship the Almighty God.

CHAPTER 6

THE BLESSING AND HONOUR IN TRUE WORSHIP

Honour

Isaiah 29:13 Therefore the Lord said: "Inasmuch as these people draw near with their mouths and honour Me with their lips, but have removed their hearts far from Me, and their fear toward Me is taught by the commandment of men."

Can we possibly worship God without honouring Him? Can honour be separated from worship?

Nope! Worship without honour is in vain.

So far we've seen that worship is essential in our relationship with God. Worship goes beyond the mere act of singing or prayer. In Isaiah 29:13 God rejected a group of worshippers because the content of their hearts didn't align with the utterances of their lips.

Singing songs of reverence and acknowledging God's greatness in prayer could be expressions of worship, but

God is calling us to something deeper and truer. A form of worship that transcends these traditionally accepted acts of worship.

Jesus says in **John 4:23-24 But the hour is coming, and now is, when the true worshipers will worship the Father in spirit and truth; for the Father is seeking such to worship Him. Vs. 24 God is Spirit, and those who worship Him must worship in spirit and truth.**

God is seeking people who will worship Him in Spirit and in truth, which is the only acceptable form of worship in His sight.

Romans 12:1-2 I beseech you therefore, brethren, by the mercies of God, that you present your bodies a living sacrifice, holy, acceptable to God, which is your reasonable service. 2 And do not be conformed to this world, but be transformed by the renewing of your mind, that you may prove what is that good and acceptable and perfect will of God.

To worship God is to honour Him, that is, to reverence and preference His will. Honour is a state of consciousness and submission to God's sovereignty. This means that worship is a total surrender of our being. In other words, we must be willing to surrender all our human faculties, our minds, emotions, intellect and will to Him.

So worshiping God is ideally living out **Proverbs 3:5-6 Trust in the Lord with all your heart, and lean not on your own understanding; Vs.6 In all your ways acknowledge Him, and He shall direct your paths**. When we lean on our own understanding, it means we are not worshipping God and that is an act of dishonour. If we are worshipping God or living in true worship, our hearts must constantly be in search and practice of what pleases Him.

What does the Word of God say concerning this situation? What does He want me to say or think? Are my actions pleasing to Him?

And this is why we must renew our minds by studying the Word of God and also consistently yield to the promptings of the Holy Spirit.

John 14:26 But the Helper, the Holy Spirit, whom the Father will send in My name, He will teach you all things, and bring to your remembrance all things that I said to you.

So if you really wish to honour God in worship then we must adopt His preferences. This is what it means to offer your body as a living sacrifice unto Him and this is what He regards as true and proper worship.

The Blessing

Genesis 12:1-5 Now the Lord had said to Abram:
"Get out of your country,
From your family
And from your father's house,
To a land that I will show you.
Vs.2 I will make you a great nation;
I will bless you
And make your name great;
And you shall be a blessing.
Vs.3 I will bless those who bless you,
And I will curse him who curses you;

And in you all the families of the earth shall be blessed."
Vs.4- So Abram departed as the Lord had spoken to him, and Lot went with him. And Abram was seventy-five years old when he departed from Haran. Vs.5- Then Abram took Sarai his wife and Lot his brother's son, and *all their possessions that*

they had gathered, **and the people whom they had acquired in Haran, and they departed to go to the land of Canaan.**

So they came to the land of Canaan.

Abraham was an idol worshipper who heard God's call, heard the gospel preached, and responded. Abraham was told to leave his father's house in Haran and travel to Canaan, a land where God led him and promised to make him a blessing to the entire planet. So today, we're discussing Abraham's blessing.

Remember that the Bible is a book of salvation, and any terms used in it must be related to God's plan of salvation. When you hear Abraham's blessings or the song: *Abraham's blessings are mine...'*, please don't think of money, a car, a house, or a spouse.

Remember Abraham was already a wealthy man; he was already very rich before God called him. How do we know that **Genesis 13:2-3 Abram was very rich in livestock, in silver, and in gold. Vs.3- And he went on his journey from the South as far as Bethel, to the place where his tent had been at the beginning, between Bethel and Ai,**

Abraham was already very wealthy before embarking on the journey to the Promised Land. Genesis 13:2 states that Abraham was wealthy in livestock, silver, and gold, even before receiving God's call or leaving Haran for Canaan. Abraham had all of that. Abraham was not a poor man before he came to God. So the blessing God is referring to here is neither money, nor house, nor car or spouse. The blessing God is referring to here is none of the material stuff.

The Hebrew word for blessing is *"BERAKAH."* For Abraham, this term had no connection to his material possessions. Instead, the blessing signified justification by faith, righteousness without works. The Bible notes that Abraham believed in God, and it was counted to him as righteousness.

Romans 4:1-3 NIV What then shall we say that Abraham, our forefather according to the flesh, discovered in this matter? Vs.2 If, in fact, Abraham was justified by works, he had something to boast about — but not before God. Vs.3 What does Scripture say? "Abraham believed God, and it was credited to him as righteousness."

To understand the word blessing, let us look at the story in **Genesis 27:8-13**

Now therefore, my son, obey my voice according to what I command you. Vs.9- Go now to the flock and bring me from there two choice kids of the goats, and I will make savoury food from them for your father, such as he loves. Vs.10- Then you shall take it to your father, that he may eat it, and that he may bless you before his death." Vs.11- And Jacob said to Rebekah his mother, "Look, Esau my brother is a hairy man, and I am a smooth – skinned man. Vs.12- Perhaps my father will feel me, and I shall seem to be a deceiver to him; and I shall bring a curse on myself and not a blessing." V.13 But his mother said to him, "Let your curse be on me, my son; only obey my voice, and go, get them for me."

This was when Rebecca was telling Jacob to pretend to be Esau and go to his blind father Isaac and collect the blessing that was meant for Esau. Then Jacob said to his mother. **"My father will discover that it is me Jacob and he will instead curse me"**

but his mother, Rebecca, said, **"Let the curse be upon me"**. Jacob craftily went to Isaac and obtained the blessing. Esau later returned with the soup he had prepared for his father. Isaac said to Esau, **"Your brother came subtly and has taken away your blessing"**. Jacob had not taken away the inheritance; he had not taken away the house; he had not taken away the money. If it were the car, the money, or the house, the elder brother would have gone after him and collected it. Remember, the elder brother Esau was a skilled hunter. Esau could have hunted Jacob down and collected the car, the house, or the money. That means what Jacob had taken away is something that cannot be collected.

The blessing is not tangible; the blessing is intangible. The blessing is nothing tangible; the blessing is immaterial. Esau showed up after his father had prayed and laid his hands on Jacob. When you come to the New Testament, you will call prayer and laying of hands as impactation and ordination. That is why Esau could not go to collect it because it is not something collectable. Isaac laid his hands on Jacob; he came close to him, so we say he ministered to him in the New Testament language.

When Jacob was gone, Esau now came in **Gen 27:37-38 Then Isaac answered and said to Esau, "indeed I have made him your master, and all his brethren I have**

given to him as servants; with grain and wine I have sustained him. What shall I do now for you, my son?" Vs.38 And Esau said to his father, "Have you only one blessing, my father? Bless me — me also, O my father!" And Esau lifted up his voice and wept.

Isaac insisted 'I have blessed him and he shall be blessed'. Even your coming cannot change it. I have already blessed Jacob; now that you have arrived, let me reaffirm and emphasize that your brother Jacob is blessed. The blessing is irreversible. Once God bestows His blessing upon you, which you got at redemption, it is irreversible. Nobody can take God's blessing from you.

In the shadows, in the Old Testament, there is the fascinating story of Balak and Balaam's failed attempt to curse Israel. God stopped them and said **"...you shall not curse the people, for they are blessed." Numbers 22:12**

What God gives is **permanent**. We have the chorus of a gospel song that goes like this: *"It shall be permanent, it shall be permanent, what the Lord has done for us, it shall be permanent"*

Ephesians 1:3 KJV Blessed be the God and Father of our Lord Jesus Christ, who hath blessed us with all spiritual blessings in heavenly places in Christ.

You and I, know that money is not permanent, so money cannot be a blessing. A car is not permanent, so a car cannot be a blessing. A house is not permanent either; it depreciates. Even a spouse is not permanent; he or she may die or even marry another. Anytime we say to you that 'God will bless you or you are blessed', do not think of material things. Think about spiritual stuff.

"The blessing is immaterial. Isaac found out that he had prophesied by the spirit to the second son, Jacob, and not to the first son, Esau. Isaac prophesied and spoke words of the spirit into the life of the second son instead of the first son, Esau.

But the argument comes that the second son lied, but he still got the blessings. Much later, Jacob will come back and repent of his deceit.

Birth right and blessing will deal with functioning in your father's office, in his inheritance, and in his possession. That is the meaning of birth right when this event took place.

Functioning in your father's office, wealth, and legacy is a spiritual activity. Who was Isaac, and who was his father? His father was Abraham. And who was Abraham? Abraham was a prophet or God's spokesman, known as *'Nabir'* in Hebrew. In their culture, and as you may know, this still goes on in our African cultures. When a man has a traditional post or title, he passes it down to his son, usually the first son, like the chief or king of a village.

So, as it usually happened, it was expected that Ishmael, Abraham's first son, would receive the blessing, but unexpectedly, it went to Isaac. Similarly, it was anticipated in the book of Genesis that it would be Cain, not Abel, who would receive the blessing, but contrary to expectations, the blessing went to Abel. This unexpected turn of events is because the story of Genesis is fundamentally about God's Grace and not about works. So, by Grace, it is not Cain; it is Abel. It is not Ishmael; it is Isaac. It is not Esau; it is Jacob—God's grace, God's unmerited favour. By Grace, men began to occupy the esteemed office of the prophet, or men began to become ministers of God's word in the earth. That is the birth right or the blessing. The blessing is to be called into a privileged office to preach the gospel.

The blessing is to be called into the mandate of God as a representative of Jesus Christ. Naturally, it should have fallen on Esau, the first son, but that is not how it works. It works by Grace, not by works lest any man should boast. It is the gift of God. So, it falls on Jacob, not Esau. The Bible is not talking about money, houses and cars when it refers to the blessing. When you read the book of Genesis, you see that Cain was a very wealthy man without the blessing. Under the curse, Cain was very rich; he built a city, and his children began to make inventions, owning cities.

Cain, who was operating under a curse, was still very wealthy. It is only in Africa that we have this misconception that when you are poor, you say you are cursed, whereas the first man that was under a curse in the Bible was Cain and he was wealthy under the curse. Because the curse is nothing material. The curse is not to be received into God's grace. The blessing is to be welcomed into the grace of God and the ministry of the gospel. The blessing is that office you have as a child of God to minister Christ to unbelievers and to bring the light of the gospel and salvation to lost souls. The blessing is the office of the minister of the gospel, bringing the good news to lost souls. The blessing is the privilege we have today to be ambassadors of Christ and be light in a world of darkness. In the blessing, we worship God in spirit and truth (in reality).

The Blessing & Honour

Now let's look at the connection between the blessing and honour in worship.

Genesis 25: 29-34 Now Jacob cooked a stew; and Esau came in from the field, and he was weary.

Vs.30 And Esau said to Jacob, "Please feed me with that same red stew, for I am weary." Therefore, his name was called Edom.Vs.31 But Jacob said, "Sell me your birth right as of this day." Vs.32 And Esau said, "Look, I am about to die; so what is this birth right to me?"

Vs.33 Then Jacob said, "Swear to me as of this day." So he swore to him, and sold his birth right to Jacob. Vs.34 And Jacob gave Esau bread and stew of lentils; then he ate and drank, arose, and went his way.Thus Esau despised his birth right.

In Genesis chapter 25, the scripture recorded the conversation between Jacob and Esau, where Jacob asked

Esau for his birth right to exchange for a plate of soup. Listen to what Esau said "Who cares about birth right? I am hungry. Did you say that if I say from now on, you are the firstborn and I am the last born, you will give me a bowl of porridge?"

See the response of Jacob: "Yes, if you agree, then from today, I will take over your place in this family and I will give you the plate of porridge. Then Esau said "What is first born, give me food and take it".

What is the call of God to ministry? Give me food and take your call of God away. What is all this talk about the call of God in my life? Let me just make the money, own material wealth and forget about God. Does the call of God put food on my table?

Such thinking shows that you are a person who doesn't understand honour. It also means you haven't understood what it truly means to be blessed.

Esau sold his birth right for a plate of soup, and the Bible labelled him a profane man. Eventually, he would realize that forfeiting the birth right meant relinquishing the blessing. Once the birth right is given away via dishonour, the blessing goes with it. Similarly, declining

God's call to ministry or service as a Christian equates to refusing the blessing. Esau should have esteemed the blessing and recognized the value of honouring God.

The blessing, in this context, involves being called by God to preach the gospel — a responsibility not exclusive to pastors only but applicable to all born-again Christians. As a medical doctor, I emphasize that even in my profession, I am compelled to preach the gospel.

Romans10:13-15 For "Everyone who calls on the name of the Lord will be saved." Vs.14 But how can they call on him to save them unless they believe in him? And how can they believe in him if they have never heard about him? And how can they hear about him unless someone tells them? Vs.15 And how will anyone go and tell them without being sent?

That is why the Scriptures say, *"How beautiful are the feet of messengers who bring good news!"*

We are saved (blessed) to be a blessing to others until all the families of the earth are blessed (saved). The blessing is in the preaching of the gospel, the divine call to evangelize, and the mandate to raise disciples across the earth's expanse. It entails being an ambassador of the message of Christ.

Esau, identified as a profane man, held little regard for spiritual matters. Today, many individuals share a similar disposition to Esau, treating spiritual gifts with casualness. The call of God should never be taken lightly, as disdain for it hinders its flow. What one despises, one cannot fully enjoy. Let us serve God's purpose for our generation every day of our lives by honouring Him through true worship.

Say this to yourself; *"There is a call of God on my life and I refuse to give the devil room at any juncture in my life. I know there is a mandate, there is an assignment, there is a mission of God on earth and that mission of God on earth has been conferred on me. I am a carrier of the blessing and I will honour my Lord."*

CHAPTER 7

MEDICAL BENEFITS OF THE TRUE WORSHIP OF GOD

Incorporating the true worship of God into your daily life is essential. Moreover, it is crucial to consider the vast array of medical benefits associated with this practice. The physical benefits become even more noteworthy as we continually engage in worship. True worship not only provides a spiritual connection but also presents an opportunity for improved health and wellness, both mentally and physically, which, in turn, leads to an enhanced quality of life and potentially a longer life span.

Worship is indispensable for fostering better psychological health, bolstering a healthier immune system, reducing stress levels, enhancing mood, and facilitating a more functional metabolism.

The regular and sincere worship of God brings forth the following undeniable and concrete medical benefits:

1. *Regulates heart rate and promotes effective breathing.*

As we engage in worship, the sympathetic nervous system—which triggers the fight-or-flight response—slows down, allowing the parasympathetic nervous system to induce a restful and rejuvenating state. This will lead to a decrease in blood pressure, a steadier heart rate, and improved rate and depth of breathing, collectively promoting cardiovascular health and respiratory efficiency while reducing the risk of heart-related ailments. So we see that worship contributes to the development of a stronger cardiovascular and respiratory system.

2. *Relieves stress, improves mental health and plays a significant role in chronic pain relief.*

Engaging in true worship releases the body's natural 'feel-good' chemicals or hormones called endorphins while reducing cortisol levels, a hormone commonly associated with stress. This will significantly lower stress levels while fostering feelings of joy and positivity, which in turn leads to a noticeable improvement in the mental health of the worshiper and better cognitive resilience to deal with the stresses of daily life. Also, engaging in worship can trigger the body 's endogenous analgesic pathways thus playing a significant role in the management and relief of chronic pain. We mentioned earlier that worship has been linked to the release of endorphins. These feel good chemicals are also the body's natural analgesics which are crucial in alleviating pain perception as well as improving overall pain management. Medical studies conducted by Amy B Wachholtz et al (2005) and Katja Wiech et al (2008), highlight the neurochemical mechanisms at work and show how worship can be a powerful way to release endogenous painkillers. This implies that a true worshipper has a greater threshold for pain and this may aid in faster recovery following medical procedures.

3. *Enhances the immune system effectively.*

A healthy immune system is crucial for defending the body against illnesses and pathogens. Engaging in worship has been linked to increased production of immune-boosting cells and proteins such as immunoglobulins and leukocytes which are necessary for a robust immune system. Positive emotions such as gratitude, love and peace are frequently evoked by worship and it's surprising to learn that these feelings are vital for immune support. In addition, true worshippers turn to have better lifestyle choices and social behaviours which have been linked to improved immunity. Collectively, these factors may support and optimize the body's ability to fend off illnesses.

All these therapeutic and medical benefits work together to provide us with enhanced physical health as we engage in a lifestyle of true worship of God.

ABOUT THE BOOK

In Divine Prescriptions: Exploring the Spiritual and Medical benefits of Worship, Dr. Paul Atem delves into a profound exploration of genuine worship, drawing insights from the teachings of Jesus Christ and examining its roots in the Old Testament through types and shadows. The narrative seamlessly weaves together these elements, providing a contextual understanding of what it truly means to worship God in Spirit and Truth, as emphasized in the New Testament. Notably, Dr. Atem takes a unique approach by delving into the medical benefits of true worship, adding a distinctive spiritual and medical dimension to the book.

ABOUT THE AUTHOR

As a christian Medical Doctor, Dr. Atem brings a wealth of expertise and experience to his analysis. Serving as the proprietor and medical director of the Pro-life Mount Zion Clinic in Bamenda, Cameroon, he has dedicated himself to both spiritual and physical well-being. Additionally, Dr. Atem holds the role of proprietor for the Mount Zion University Higher Institute in Bamenda and Buea.

Dr. Atem's commitment to his faith and profession is reflected not only in his insightful exploration of worship but also in his personal life. He shares a joyous marriage with his beautiful wife, Comfort, and they are blessed with four children: Emmanuel, Peace, Favour, and Joshua. This personal touch adds warmth to the narrative, showcasing the integration of faith, family, and medical expertise in Dr. Atem's life.

CONTACT INFORMATION

Dr. Paul Atem

P.O.BOX 246

Vicky Street,

Bamenda,

Cameroon,

Africa

Tel: +237- 677770177

WhatsApp: +237- 676375537

Email: dratempaul2015@gmail.com

www.ingramcontent.com/pod-product-compliance
Lightning Source LLC
Chambersburg PA
CBHW071550120726

48009CB00007B/247/J